Christianity

&

The

Writer's

Task

GEORGES BERNANOS

EDITED BY JOHN-PAUL HEIL

Wiseblood Books

Copyright © 2022 Wiseblood Books

All rights reserved, including the right to reproduce this book or any portions thereof in any form whatsoever except for brief quotations in book reviews. For information, address the publisher:

> Wiseblood Books
> P.O. Box 870
> Menomonee Falls, WI 53052

Printed in the United States of America

Set in Baskerville Typesetting
Cover Design: Silk Sheep Studio

Paperback ISBN-13: 978-1-951319-53-3

CONTENTS

CHRISTIANITY AND THE WRITER'S TASK:
LETTER TO FRÉDÉRIC LEFÈVRE

1

JOURNAL ENTRIES AND LETTERS RECOUNTING
AN ECCLESIAL EXISTENCE

13

SERMON OF AN AGNOSTIC ON
THE FEAST OF ST. THÉRÈSE

37

Acknowledgements

"Christianity and the Writer's Task: Letter to Frédéric Lefèvre"

> *Communio* obtained foreign permission to translate and reprint this essay from: *Essais et écrits de combat*, vol. 1 (Paris: Gallimard, 1971), 1048–55.

"Journal Entries and Letters Recounting an Ecclesial Existence"

> The selections translated in this article appear in a German-language anthology edited by Hans Urs von Balthasar under the title *Georges Bernanos. Das sanfte Erbarmen: Briefe des Dichters* (Einsiedeln: Johannes Verlag, 1951). Parts of *Communio*'s translation by Adrian Walker were taken from Balthasar's *Bernanos: An Ecclesial Existence* (San Francisco: Ignatius Press, 1996).

"Sermon of an Agnostic on the Feast of St. Thérèse"

> This article is part of a selection of the writings of Georges Bernanos published by William B. Eerdmans Publishing Co. as part of the *Ressourcement* series: *The Heroic Face of Innocence: Three Stories* (Grand Rapids: Eerdmans, 1999), 23–38.

We wish to express our heartfelt thanks to the editors of *Communio*, especially managing editor Ms. Carmen Ferre Martí, for granting us permission to republish these selections, each of which originally appeared in its pages:

> Georges Bernanos, "Christianity and the Writer's Task: Letter to Frédéric Lefèvre," trans. David Christopher Schindler, *Communio* 28, no. 1 (Spring 2001): 202–10.

Georges Bernanos, "Journal Entries and Letters Recounting an Ecclesial Existence," trans. Adrian Walker, *Communio* 23, no. 2 (Summer 1996): 374–88.

Georges Bernanos, "Sermon of an Agnostic on the Feast of St. Thérèse," trans. Pamela Morris and David Louis Schindler, Jr., *Communio* 24, no. 3 (Fall 1997): 611–22.

CHRISTIANITY AND THE WRITER'S TASK

BY

GEORGES BERNANOS

Letter to Frédéric Lefèvre[1]

My dear friend,

You insist that I tell you more about my book.[2] Your friendship, whose generous devotion I can attest better than anyone else, merits this little sacrifice. But sincere books aren't the easiest to defend, and you know that I wrote this one with an imprudent good faith. Being forced to earn my living by insuring that of others, I spend the larger part of my time in hotels or train stations.[3] A page here, a page there, scribbled under a cloud of pipe smoke, in the midst of an innocent storm unleashed by cardplayers, under a cashier's fixed stare. When a person tears a book out of himself like this, one line at a time, there can be no doubt that the book is sincere—he didn't have enough time to compose himself before the mirror! . . . But this is also the way a person opens himself up for surprises. The moment it appeared, this book caused a certain scandal.

Of course, I do not feel the same level of interest toward each of the scandalized parties. There exists a certain bitter truth that no one wishes to look in the face, and there are, for example, certain priests who are full of

---

1. Translated by David Christopher Schindler.

2. Bernanos is referring to his novel *Sous le Soleil de Satan (Under Satan's Sun)*, which appeared in 1926. —Translator.

3. In order to support his family, Bernanos worked as a traveling life insurance salesman. —Tr.

artifice and guile, and who would happily let these scandalized souls fade into oblivion were it not that Providence conducted them with a motherly indulgence, one by one, into literary salons or even into the Academy, and thus carried them quickly out of harm's way. Nor do I feel much pity for the pious people who, one might say, form part of the liturgical furniture, and whose intellectual servility is enough to bring the Angels to despair. Take this lackey, for example, who answers to the name of Mangolf. Puffed up with decency and wind, he reproaches me for "Fr. Donissan's dry leather shoes, his dirty cassock, and his lack of posture and style," which, this terrific fool explains, is incompatible with the lights of the twentieth century . . . And he is not the only such fool.

I would despair about ever reaching them, except perhaps by writing another book. Author's prefaces have always struck me as somewhat idiotic, but what can you say about attempts to explain oneself! And yet it happens that a letter persuades me to break my silence, because it is one of those letters that one not only reads, but listens to, a letter that contains a sincere outcry. You know which letter I am speaking about, because you were the one who brought it to me: it was addressed to you, and signed by Gaston Leroux. The subtle and haunted novelist, who wrote *Parfum de la dame en noire*, has gone much more deeply into my book than many people who pretend they have. But, in my opinion, he followed the path in the opposite direction, and took my point of departure for a point of arrival.

An author in bad faith will defend himself by means of texts, which are always easy to solicit. As for me, I will simply explain my intentions—and these are not empty words! It is true that the war has forced us to revise our moral values from top to bottom. It is undeniably true that we have been moved to revulsion, that we have grown sick and tired of the *mystique*, the religion of the goddess France and Saint Poilu,[4] which the mighty newspapers have been serving up to this poor, overtaxed people.

This disgust, which for us has become quite lucid, has been felt in a more unconscious way by a great number of people. The palpable tribulation of war awoke in more than a few souls what I would call the tragic sense of life, the need to enter into a relation with the great laws of the spiritual universe, to integrate the great human misfortune back into the spiritual order. The problem of Life is the problem of Suffering.

But this is where the moralist leaves off. The groaning wrenched from a humiliated heart is a prayer poised for birth, a spring that shoots up from soaked earth. But, alone, it is not enough. Feeling, at this initial stage, requires a support, which it finds—or believes it has—in a mystique that offers it communion with other wounded sensitivities. This, too, is a path that leads to God, but it is not the surest path. The large number of our contemporaries who end up following the suicidal naturalism of Rabindranath Tagore[5] proves it.

But, in the history of human restlessness, Rabindranath Tagore is nothing but a vivid little story. Restlessness is the unconscious source of all art, if not also the effect it inspires. To condemn this restlessness in the name of the sovereignty of reason is a vain enough endeavor. But this does not mean art does not entail certain risks. For, even

---

4. "Poilu" is the name used for French soldiers in World War I, especially those serving on the front lines. —Tr.

5. Rabindranath Tagore (1861–1941) was an Indian poet. —Tr.

in its highest and most perfect expressions, art remains a search. The work of art, even one that has been fashioned by genius, retains all the way into its sublimely tranquil heights the gesture and the form of its emergence. Yes, the sacred joy that fills us with its wondrous presence carries the sting of yearning, and our satisfied desire yields a more beautiful hope. There are some who do not and will never understand, who believe that art is made only as a vehicle of expression for a certain intellectual elite, a small troupe of clever, discerning individuals, whose cultivated taste is just another name for avarice. These people of taste, these able and judicious critics, who know how to preserve genius from certain excesses (because genius—alas!—is never fooled by halves!), they ruin everything the moment they allow themselves to play the role of experts. They do not know how to choose, and even the alternatives from which to choose they manage to find only in other people. The unconscious feeling of their impotence turns quickly to aggression, envy, and perhaps even hatred for the creative artist whom they take for an equal. Their boisterous enthusiasm thus becomes responsible for the success of some second-rate, but subtle and learned, writer, in whom they are excited to sense familiar terrain. This is how Anatole France came to be held up for everyone's admiration. Claiming to be a reaction against a new romantic anarchy, the eighteenth century tries to return to an age that predates this tired old scene. But the remedy is worse than the disease! For, the artificial intoxication of rationalism will in the end always open the way to a *delirium tremens*. And right away, in the desert of a literature gone sterile, we catch sight of the savage, the natural man, the day-dreaming primate who contemplates the total ruin of the planet with the heart of a child—Rousseau.

We cannot deny it: art has a goal that lies beyond itself. Its constant striving for expression is the faint image, or perhaps the symbol, of its unending search for Being. Would Racine, for example, ever have reached the point of perfection he did if he had not one day, in a sudden, sublime flash, gotten beyond man the moral being and rediscovered man the sinner? Nothing else, neither the silence he suddenly lapsed into nor his death, would suffice to explain the relentless bitterness, the shiver of sorrow that we perceive at every turn. No doubt, we could persuade ourselves that this fortunate rival of Corneille had learned a lesson from the exhausting battle fought by his magnanimous predecessor, and that, since he was impatient for glory, Racine passionately desired to please a public whom the author of the *Cid* had sated with sublimity and who now wanted some other amusement. But it was not with Greek or Roman sublimity that this young man dreamed of filling their yearning hearts. Indeed, what could he have conceded to popular taste if he was to say at least something about the great passions of which his stormy loves were nothing but faint images! Already in the successful, beloved, and famous adolescent's cry of victory and affirmation of life, we detect the imperceptible crack, the trembling of a joy mixed with anxiety, the search for a more urgent and profound truth. Who will follow him down the length of his arid road? To the point that he sees Phaedra suddenly appear, the woman born from his art, pale with a lust that is pushed to the extremes of torture, her tiny, hidden hand resting on the shoulder of her insignificant friend—and he recognizes a sister in her face and sees his own remorse in her dying eyes.

Moralists are boring; they interest me about as much as a small rock. If I were forced to deal with them, I would offer them someone other than my saint of Lumbres;[6] I would choose someone other than, for example, a rational saint (indeed, such exist!). But I will go further. Let me make this confession to you, Lefèvre: it is true that, out of spite, I wanted my foolish but humble and powerful hero to be a stranger to them. It pleases me that he should unsettle them. Yes, I had in mind those who reject this moralism, this attenuated Christianity, which seems to have been fashioned to fit an industrial civilization whose sole aim appears to be mastery over the material world. I wanted to say to them: "Are you looking for a vision of the moral world that is both logical and emotional? Look no further."

I believe that my book will initially scandalize precisely those to whom it has something to give. Those baptized individuals who have retained from their forgotten catechism only the vague memory of a collection of rules or imaginative symbols meant to facilitate the observance of moral precepts. God keeps watch over us above the ages and he shows a fatherly smile to those sins whose vanity he knows. The devil is an undisciplined fellow who plays out childish farces before the inaccessible Trinity. People tolerate the saint as long as he is a humanitarian, but he is looked on as a lunatic the moment he steps beyond the limits of bourgeois prudence. The sister of charity is loved for keeping kids' noses wiped; but the moment she enters Carmel, she becomes for some a fanatic, and, for the more indulgent others, a rare flower, an ornament, a precious human trinket . . . But what is all this? What does this have to do with the crucified Christ?

My dear Lefèvre, I have figured out what it is that lies

---

6. The protagonist of *Sous le Soleil de Satan,* Fr. Donissan, is referred to as the "saint of Lumbres." —Tr.

behind the touching surprise of M. Gaston Leroux. He attributes one cause or another to the terror that suddenly gripped him. But what he says doesn't matter. I know better than he what I have stirred; I am familiar with this precise point, this vital core, in the soul. *I have taught M. Gaston Leroux what sin is.*

The problem of Life, I was saying, is the problem of Suffering. But that wasn't quite right. The whole of the problem of Life can find ample space inside the problem of Sin. What is Sin, then? Is it the transgression of the law? It is indeed, but what a poor abstraction that notion is! Instead, we learn everything we need to know about sin when we call it by its proper name: it is deicide, the murder of God.

I know that this is a hard word. It is so convenient to picture a Creator who smiles at his creature's mix-ups, or perhaps wrinkles his brow! But if you leave anything at all out of this primary definition, redemption loses all of its meaning, and the ignominious agony of the Just One becomes nothing but a horrid and senseless story.

On a similar topic, moreover, human language has multiplied ambiguity. Its essential cowardice is nowhere more apparent. It says or writes: "Evil" [*Mal*]. This word is used indifferently of suffering and of sin, of crime and of that which is precisely its unspeakable compensation.[7] The rational animal has pulled off the feat of enclosing both the idea of deicide and that of a powerful flair of tooth pain within the very same abstract sign.

Sin is the murder of God, my dear M. Leroux, and I confess that this mystery is difficult to get beyond: indeed,

---

7. The French word *mal* is far more general than the English "evil;" it can stand for everything from "evil" *per se* to "harm," "pain," or "discomfort." —Tr.

we are not asked to do as much. But, inscrutable as it is in its essence, this mystery justifies itself enough by reestablishing order in the moral universe, by bringing to a unity elements that have been up to this point irreducible, by giving to the problem of suffering an equitable solution. When sin was nothing but the breaking of a law, such a severe repression of sin was incomprehensible. But it is in the first place a crime against Love. The sacrifice of the Cross is not only a compensatory sacrifice, because justice is no longer the only thing involved, it is not only justice that has been outraged. To a crime against Love, Love responds in its own way and according to its own nature: by a total, infinite gift. Where will the union between Creator and creature, between victim and executioner, take place? In the suffering that is common to them both.

We stand at the center of this prodigious drama, we are at the very heart of the Most Holy Trinity. What does it mean? To be inside God himself, inside his incomprehensible hurricane? It seems unbelievable to you, doesn't it, since the only God you can imagine is a logician, an organizing intelligence. But this is not the first definition of God. No, God is first of all charity. He is Absolute Love. Absolute Love! Just try, by the movement of our miserable hearts, to measure such an unheard-of power! We live comfortably and unaware in the midst of this great whirlwind, and if, unimaginably, the unwavering course of its spirals were displaced to the slightest degree, entire worlds would be uprooted. For love, nothing is mediocre; everything is great. Even the tiniest part of the beloved is, for love, no less precious, urgent, or essential. Reason recoils at the first thought of this immense summons, which has rendered chaos fertile, which has carried off the most powerful of the angels as if he were a mere whisp, and which nevertheless comes to breathe its entreating, yearning, and insatiable sigh into a tiny child's ear!

M. Leroux wishes to persuade me that I have served him Despair from the bottom of my platter of hell. His testimony fills me with joy. It proves to me that I have gone beyond the limits of literature and reached the guarded depth of the soul. No doubt, there are other souls, though few (and my poor Donissan is among them) that are filled with excessive terror by a hatred of sin. I do not write *for these souls*. Nevertheless, I write about these souls, I offer their terror to the great many others who are not unworthy of the truth, but who still seek in great passions after the great message for which their hearts thirst. And, thus, what they desire is not pleasure, but suffering, which lies at the heart of what they seek. This suffering makes no sense at all, my dear Leroux, to those who see in it only the just retribution for sin. It is this, of course. But it is more than this. It is the bread that God shares with man. It is the temporal image of the possession of God to which we are all called. Why are you so afraid of such simple words, by which I try to make a basic truth visible: namely, that God asks of his friends what he himself has given—extravagant suffering? A single word could have saved us, but love follows roads unknown to reason; or rather, it joins up with reason at a place well beyond our understanding. Love needed only to give a word; but he gave his Life.

To be sure, the author of Evil is not a man. The rebel Angel said "no" just once, but he spoke it once and for all, in an irrevocable gesture in which he invested the whole of his being. Hell is no longer the place where the drama is played out; henceforth, it unfolds in the heart of the God-Man, the heart in which Humanity is rooted, the heart pierced by a lance, where our blood line opens and mingles with his, squandered without measure. For each one of us—we who are ignorant, or who understand so little!, who live like animals, completely oblivious of the sign that has marked us—there are some who suffer and who die, and it is not in vain. My poor Donissan is not completely unresponsible for the despair that drives him to martyrdom since, without realizing it, he made a sacrilegious vow. But it is in the order of things that God allows this sin to serve his own design. Isn't this what I said? Isn't this what I wrote? Even this poor soul in despair lavishes hope by the handful.

To tell the truth, I have no less contempt for the self-satisfied nonbeliever, or for the erudite priest who is able to dissertate twenty volumes on the love of God with the indifference of a collector of rare species. Let me put this more clearly: I feel contempt for the former, and the latter I detest with every fiber of my being. Who is it that accuses me of trying to make the country priest of Lumbres a saint, or even the saint? It is the simpletons who hunt through books looking for a possible novel topic. I can see one of them managing his tiny vice and his tiny virtue, raising and lowering the rates with the instincts of an old banker. Am I supposed to work for these young Scrooges? I am unable to come at either Goodness or Evil at an angle. It is impossible to live outside of reality. And reality, the positivity of life, does not consist in privileged moments of intellectual or sensual exaltation, or even vague religiosity; rather, reality is this deep expanse of suffering that suddenly bubbles to the surface like water from an underground river. But we tend to admire the people who have plugged up all of the outlets, and keep dry. Just think what an insult, what an affront to the human being this skepticism is, for example, which, as we all know, leads to the darkest of vices. It's like the old man's confidence, which started with the rarest trifles, but ends up in a sordid, evil place, where he tries in vain to stir to life something that has died within him, something that could very well be his manhood or his soul.

Journal Entries Recounting an Ecclesial Existence[1]

Notebook entry (18 January 1948)

There is a danger of imagining God's love as a kind of benevolent condescension. God longs for his creature with a desire that would pulverize us if we had even the faintest notion of it. This is why he has sunk this desire into the deepest depths of the mild, loving heart of Jesus Christ.

From a letter to a priest (1947)

. . . At bottom, the mediocrity of others keeps open a wound in us that mustn't stop festering and causing us pain; and it would close only at the risk of poisoning the whole organism. It is very nice to preach to us resignation toward others' mediocrity, when resignation threatens—as it infallibly does!—to bring with it a soothing reassurance about our own mediocrity! When the sight of mediocrity no longer tortures us, that is a sign that we ourselves have become mediocre from head to toe—unless God's gentle mercy, which is not without a sense of humor, has, unknown to us, made saints of us . . .

---

1. Translated by Adrian Walker.

Journal entry (1946)

The future will tell whether I have the words of hope. The future will tell whether each one of my books isn't a conquered despair. The old man won't resist forever; the old wreck won't eternally defy the sea; it's enough if it can withstand the wave upright to the end, and if the wave that buries it is the one that lifted it the highest.

Letters to Amoroso Lima

(1) Pirapora (January 1940)

Dear Sir,

For months I've kept putting off writing to you, all the while feeling the burden of a kind of guilt. We haven't talked very often, but even if I'd spoken to you only once with a certain heartfelt sincerity, I would be so bound to you that I could no longer treat you like just any "acquaintance" of the sort that chance ties and unties.

First of all, I wish you, as is the custom in my country, a good and happy new year. I've thought about you a great deal lately. I have no desire to wrong you in any way. I've taken myself to task as severely as possible on that score. In fact, I've forgotten neither my previous letters nor your answer, which stirred me so intensely when I first received it, although it left me in doubt as to what we might be able to give to each other. These things have a tremendous significance in my eyes, because I don't want to run my life according to conventions, not even venerable ones.

What other men expect of us is what God expects. I am quite aware that I will never succeed in conforming my life to this sublime law. But I am really convinced that this is the only thing that counts. Everything else is pious pap.

I wouldn't want you to come away from our brief meetings, which always ended up on the stormy side, with a bad impression . . . It may not have seemed like it, but I made a great effort to become a true friend to you. It's natural that you didn't notice what I was doing. The remembrance of your dead friend stood between us. I don't see him there any longer, yet this person whom I never knew is inexplicably near and dear to me. Though I leave you, I don't seem to depart from him.

It's for me to be sorry that I wasn't successful, that I wasn't able to reach you. You are at home in your country, in the most wonderful surroundings. I was alone, or rather, on the edge of solitude; I thought that I was alone, but at bottom I knew that I wasn't staying there, that no matter what I was going on—why else would I have crossed the ocean? You didn't know this. That explains a great deal and has spared us some painful misunderstandings.

We are irreconcilable, dear friend, in the way that two Christians can be; that is, we are reconcilable only in God. My hunch is that we've been like this from the time we were young. Like Mauriac and so many others, you are one of those searching, congenitally restless souls who have found a stay in a certain (somewhat abstract, I'm afraid) form of obedience and discipline, *precisely because they never felt that they were born for it*. I have never been a restless soul. Contrary to what some pitiable priests think, with all the coarseness of my nature I feel coarsely at home with obedience and discipline. In no way do these bring me the elation (or the appeasement) of a difficulty that has been overcome or a humiliation to which one has acquiesced. This is probably why I seem to make so little fuss about it. I feel at home in the Church. I'm not afraid of losing in one instant all the fruits of the efforts made to enter into the Church, because that is where I was born. Maybe that makes me unfair to those who are less coarsely secure than I am, and who want to prove to me, though they don't need to, that the house is a good one, that the priests are splendid folks, that the convents are full of selflessness and love of neighbor, that narrow sanctimoniousness is true nobility of mind, or that Pius XII's election was a blow to Mussolini, or that the cardinals who were faithful to Pius XI's policies weren't duped (the Italian technical term escapes me). All I need to know is that if this is how things are—judging by appearances and by human logic—God must have wanted it this way; that he knows what he is doing; that he no more asks us to pluck out our eyes so that we don't see what's going on than he wants us to castrate ourselves so that we can keep the sixth commandment.

Perhaps it's not worthwhile spelling all this out for you. All of it, for you and for me too, belongs to the past. They'll tell you, of course, that I clung to my opinion out of arrogance. But how could I pride myself on seeing things that are as plain as day? It is plain as day, for example, that Catholic Action was a grand idea of the pope, an idea of immense scope. It is equally plain that this kind of universal collaboration between the clergy and the laity, which was supposed to usher in a new spirit, would have appeared scandalous and revolutionary to the worthy pastors of 1880. The pastors today aren't bold enough to attack it frontally, but they certainly don't put it into effect. Sooner or later they will transform Catholic Action into a clerical action, into a federation of former parish societies or diocesan associations, all in the traditional clerical spirit. The only innovation is that they'll dress up the inveterate mediocrity of these societies with big sounding names of personalities like you who proclaim in speech and in writing what Catholic Action ought to be, so that it can continue with impunity being what it is, under the supervision of wily political priests.

We hoped that it would spark a rebirth of Christendom, of the universal Christian spirit, a rebirth that would have been vital enough to allow the head of the Church to break with the little arrangements that even their authors don't defend, but justify only with the pretext that they have to make concessions. These schemes and disavowals are daily becoming more perilous, because the press and the radio are brutally wrenching them from the shadows and exposing them to the full light of day, which they are obviously not made for. From this point of view, clerical action has become really indispensable. The idea is to form a vast Catholic mass that by its indolence and blind parroting can successfully prop up the people in charge, who find their positions jeopardized by mistakes and blunders that they are still ready to commit, less, to be sure, out of malice than out of sheer laziness to change anything. In the field of exegesis, this clerical laziness brought the Modernist crisis down on our heads. Before long we'll be seeing the result in the political field. It seems that for Catholic Action, and for every Catholic, for that matter, there remains only one completely unexceptionable activity (which, moreover, is not liable to excess): the defense of ecclesiastical authority and its methods, the rapturous exaggeration of its least successes, the concealment of its failures, even at the price of shameless lies. This work is so supremely meritorious that it justifies the most reckless interpretations even of doctrine. It's come to the point that no less than Emmanuel Mounier, the editor of the review *Esprit*, recently had to observe that:

> It would be a fundamental betrayal of our position as Christians if we identified Vatican diplomacy with the service of the faith and if, on account of this wretched subjection that is more fearful passivity than true ecclesial sense, we felt obliged to accept without criticism the acts of every nunciature and Vatican office. I am well aware that this kind of passivity is in keeping with the idea that many people have of the position of the layman in the Church. I am no less aware that it contradicts the decisive teaching and the inmost life of the Catholic Church.

When some time ago I expressed my opinion concerning the Lateran Treaty, people reproached me for lack of trust, as if I had committed a sin against faith, or something almost as bad. Recently, however, M.F. Cochin (the Cochin family certainly can't be suspected of anticlericalism!) reported with the authority of a personal friend of the deceased pope that "in his last conversations with his Milanese friends, [he, the pope] giving an example of Christian modesty, confessed that he had come to see the 'illusions and disappointments' of the first years of his reign." Flattery brings down kings, why shouldn't it ruin popes as well? You'll reply that this naive faith gives peace to simple souls. For how long? What gives you the right to let them believe that the Church gets along by miracles, that it never puts its foot down anywhere or has to take a step back, so that one day, when by some mischance the Vatican reveals itself to an unfit or unworthy person, these pitiable souls will lose their faith and imagine that they've been duped by God? As long as people obey, you say, there's no danger. You're lying, because what you say is a half-truth. What you should really say is this: as long as people obey, in free matters and because they are not in a position to form their own opinion, there is no danger. By the way, the phrase "no danger" is disgracefully anti-evangelical.

No, my dear friend, there is no such thing as a white lie [*pieux mensonge* ("pious lie")]! When the priests, presumably with the best intentions—for the clerical mentality hasn't changed—garnished our sacred texts with glosses because they wanted at all costs to fit them into their apologetical system, they had no idea that fifteen centuries later those glosses would bring the Church to the brink of the abyss and would cost her millions of souls.

I'm not trying to talk you around to my way of thinking, dear sir. In fact, I'm talking openly with you like this only to satisfy friends abroad who think that the most sensible thing I could do here is unburden my conscience once and for all. You would be perfectly entitled to retort that, since I'm not a member of Catholic Action, none of this concerns me. I would reply, once and for all, that you people are betraying an ideal obviously inspired by the Holy Spirit. Some are acting out of malice, others out of laziness, but *you are going to pay a very high price* for this betrayal of the Holy Spirit. Your confessor will laugh uproariously about this. But you, Tristan de Athayde,[2] you know very well that the judgment will not be like any of your congresses, and that the poor devils will have their say there. God knows—yes, indeed, God knows—that I

---

2. Lima's pen name. —Tr.

don't feel called to be the witness for the prosecution. But when I'm asked to give testimony, I'll do so according to my conscience and to the degree of scandal that I'm given.

Forgive me this long letter. Forget it. Don't let me trouble you. I've found what I was looking for in Brazil. Here I am today, trying to speak, as worthily as I possibly can, in my journal about the solitude of men of good will.[3] So it would have been a kind of irony on the part of the good Lord if at the same time he had heaped warm acceptance and friendship on me. The Catholic circles have given me what they have to give to someone who doesn't flatter them: nothing. Understandably, they have nothing to say to an author who twice—after the *Sun*[4] and again after *Diary of a Country Priest*—sacrificed the material profit of a best seller to what he considered his duty; an author who twice purposely gave up a large readership from which he could have gotten honor and fortune if he had only made a few concessions. The only thing I'll take away from here is the pitiful vituperation (that I know about only from hearsay) of an obscure paper in Bello Horizonte. There was apparently nothing to respond to, otherwise you would have written a response.

God's grace be with you, dear friend. Or rather, what I once wrote to Charles Maurras (when he had been reconciled by Franco): God's sweet mercy!

Your Friend,
Georges Bernanos

---

3. The journal would be published later as *Les enfants humiliés*. —Tr.

4. *Sous le Soleil de Satan.* —Tr.

(2) Pirapora (1 March 1940)

My dear Lima,

When I don't answer letters, it's because I'm lazy, and not at all because I'm a genius. Oh my, you're forming a very literary picture of me! And of my solitude too! . . . By the way, where do you get the idea that solitude alienates one from people and makes it hard to understand them? Looking at it as a Christian, even as a human being, I would have supposed the opposite. In silence and aloneness you find yourself, and this truth gives you access to the truth of others. Mixing with people every day, no matter how much goodwill you might apply, doesn't teach us much more than their weaknesses, their bad habits, their quirks, their superficiality. Besides, it encourages us in that loathsome attitude of benevolent indulgence that so many priests flitting about their parish guilds shamelessly declare is the same as love. It teaches us much less to serve men than to make use of them. But those who would make use of men, even for the most uplifting ends, run a tremendous risk. You certainly don't want to say that it isn't necessary to avoid this risk at any price; that we merely shouldn't take it upon ourselves without need, on the assumption that Providence is obliged to make up for our blunders; that we'll even end up with a few merits to our credit, albeit at the expense of the poor devils on whom we have tested our formulas and who have served us as guinea pigs.

You cannot play with men for whom Christ died. You can no more play with men and go unpunished than you can with God.

There is, it is true, another solitude than the kind I mean, a sort of solitude which is nothing but a deserter's pride born of arrogance and contempt. I honestly do not believe that this is my solitude; it wouldn't have allowed me to write *Diary of a Country Priest* or *Joy*—don't you agree? So leave these conjectures to some of those Brazilian priests of yours who thrive in fat city parishes while handing their wretched country-folk over to foreign missionaries.

No, my friend, you are wrong when you write to me that you "have nothing to tell me [Bernanos] that I don't know already." You have a great deal to tell me—me, or someone else who is worthier of hearing it than I am—a great deal that you have never admitted even to yourself and that nonetheless radiates from you at times.

By the way, your letter doesn't fool me. I can feel that you have pulled back, or that someone has pulled you back. Nothing is further from my mind, nothing is more hateful to me, than indiscretion in matters of the interior life. Don't hesitate, then, to break off this correspondence if you think you should. Realize that for me this is not a game, nor an opportunity to add to my good deeds. I haven't any. Let's not sink to the level of stimulating chatter. If you truly want to descend from your intelligence, then you have to keep your end of this Pascalian wager. For you are, after all, a leader, a teacher, a director of souls. It is not right for you to charm your adherents into the dubious security of willed stupidity, or to keep them in it, while you reserve for yourself the right to back out of it when, in your judgment, the occasion requires. Allow me to remind you that for a man of your stamp, of your formation, willed stupidity can be just as fascinating an experience as the brown bread tramps eat can be for a millionaire. You mustn't trifle with the brown bread of those tramps, who for their part wouldn't mind experiencing a taste of *foie gras* and Burgundy.

There is a passage in your letter which hurt me, not on my account, I assure you, but for your sake. How could I have spoken in such a bantering tone of the abyss I had slid by if that abyss had been heresy? I simply meant that I had occasionally been tempted to leave the clergy to that comfortable mediocrity of theirs, to write novels à la Mauriac that would have earned me a lot of money, and to live a merry little life like any other former pupil of the Jesuits. I find it monstrous that you so naively made yourself guilty of such an outrageous judgment, whereas you would hardly have dared think me capable of not paying my tailor's bill. It could be that you let your friends know about your (or my) letter and took the occasion to repeat to them this unfounded conjecture of yours. In that case, it is my duty to request that you enlighten the persons concerned.

It's really funny that, after having read my books, you could imagine me discussing with theologians some point of the doctrine of the Fathers or in conciliar decisions. No, dear friend, they're abusing your well-intentioned renunciation of your mind when they try to convince you that, if I'm fed up with hearing Russian atrocities in Finland condemned for the same reason that oppression in Spain was once sanctioned, it's because I have an arrogant spirit.

The bishops' excuse or justification when they appear before the good Lord will be to say to him, "Lord, it all served my policies, our political interests, and it never caused our pious faithful any scandal. Catholic opinion helped us along this path."

Forgive me for speaking with a certain bitterness. I'm fighting against sadness today, and anxiety is eating me up. A storm is passing right over us and it's thundering like God himself. What joy there is in the world, what joyous raging, what raging joy! Wow, the mountains are frisking like lambs! It seems to me that I've gradually learned to contemplate this joy in humility. It isn't created for me, it doesn't know me. But I know it, and I love it.

It is splendid to be able to tell you, in spite of everything, that, lost in this abyss of universal joy, human pain continues talking to the good Lord with the same gentle voice—man's sweet pain, so deliberate, so patient and always so attentively concerned to carry out its task until the very end, until everything is at an end, until the naive coming of glory, until the first morning.

Your old friend,
Georges Bernanos

(3) Pirapora (13 March 1940)

Dear Friend,

I've just received today, the 13th, your letter of the 6th, and this idiotic postal delay didn't even leave me enough time to answer you from Bello Horizonte. No matter.

The tone of your letter, so simple, moved me in the same way that I used to be moved in that peaceful house in Petropolis. Then, as now, this state hardly admits of an explanation, of a full justification. It is a movement of the soul towards you, as if I were waking up after a long discussion with you in a dream without having retained anything of our imaginary conversation.

I've always been sorry that I never answered your first letter, or rather, I still don't know whether I did well or ill in leaving your letter unanswered. I've certainly never wished to appear "sympathetic" to you—to use a word frequently employed in this country, in a sense that isn't mine. I would rather just accept the fact that I was going to repel or wound you than meet you anywhere else than where God has chosen. It is true that I am (perhaps it's just an impression) criss-crossed by contradictory feelings towards you, but at least you've never been a matter of indifference to me. To put it briefly, I've had a lot of disappointments in Brazil. I know today that the only real disappointment would be one that came from you. Don't be angry because I put this in the conditional. Think instead of everything that protects you; not, of course, against all possible disappointments, but against the most violent blows that they might bring. Think of your activity, your relations, of everything that you have to distract you every day from yourself, from the hurting part of yourself. And there is no doubt, for example, that you love your country. But it is a childlike country, its responsibilities are those of a child; all its missteps can be made good again. Whereas my country is presently playing a game whose stakes are its life and soul, not only its life, but something worth a thousand times more than its life: its mission, its eternal salvation. Realize that the sort of existence that I've fashioned for myself leaves me no other refuge from pain than the one I find in myself, that is, in the measure of strength, courage and clear-sightedness that God deigns to grant me.

And I too, my friend, am playing for my mission and my life. You will counter that these are rather grand words to say about myself; but the really grand words are like the really grand lords, in that they never forget their station. Our missions are what they are; *they are*, that is all; they are entrusted to us. And I don't believe that we can be released from them any more easily than a religious can be released from his vows. Oh, to be sure, some sly Jesuit brother, crammed with experience of worldly men like an old pipe stuffed with tobacco, may have a good laugh over what I'm saying here. For him, a "writer" is presumably a "literarily gifted" type, one who carried off prizes for essay-writing in high school and who must have said to himself one day that his "fluent pen" promised him a "brilliant career," admission to the "best circles" and some day—who knows?—thanks to the ardent prayers of a Christian wife, a seat in the *Académie Française*. That isn't how I look at the matter. I didn't appoint myself to be a writer, I became one very late and not exactly willingly. I also believe that success hasn't gone to my head or intoxicated me. What would I get intoxicated with anyway? I've always lived in my home country as you now see me living in yours; I don't seem to be the sort of person who pushes ahead in the world. In short, I believe that I've shown the proper regard for my mission; it hasn't been a source of honors and advantages for me, I haven't treated it like a mistress,[5] but like an esteemed companion to whom God has joined me. We have to attain our salvation together, not by abstinence, by continence, but by consummating each other to the very end, one by means of the other, do you see? To do what one is not called to do—even if it were to collect merits (at least so long as one hasn't delivered oneself into the hands of legitimate superiors, in the framework of the religious life)—is just as undignified and inhuman as to marry without love in order to avoid temptations against the sixth commandment by going through the weekly marital acrobatics. Those are abominable perversions of gospel renunciation at the hands of the realistic Pharisees. I add that if I wanted to act out for myself the farce of a certain simplicity, I would be nothing more than a fraud; I would be acting like someone who can't read or write so as not to be judged on what I've read or written. Yet I still couldn't outwit the good Lord. There's no other way: my mission, my work, my life have to be a whole, and I have to lift up this whole to him. Devotional exercises alone won't save me. Now, don't think that I disdain them. I pray my rosary every day like any pious old lady, I read my Mass every day (because I don't have the opportunity to hear it),

---

5. In French, "mission" is feminine. —Tr.

I never lay down to sleep without having prayed compline. But I don't consider that my duty is done because of that. I know that it would be less dangerous to be an ordinary craftsman like our beloved Saint Joseph. But Christian life is always a tremendous risk, dear friend, and not an uplifting gimmick. This is what I think.

Now I've let myself be led astray into writing you a very long letter. I believe that you don't know me very well.

I thank you once again, very fraternally, for your sympathy. Pray for me.

Most cordially yours,
Georges Bernanos

(4) Palacio Hotel, Av. Alfonso Penna
—Bello Horizonte (June 1940)

Dear Friend,

I wasn't able to meet you in Rio, but I hope to return there soon—*si Dias quizer* [God willing].

Your letter sought me in Pirapora, a couple of days after my departure for Bello Horizonte. My children sent it after me, and it waited for me there until I got back from Rio. I found it when I got to the hotel.

I thank you for thinking of me. I thank you above all and with my whole soul for having responded so quickly and so nobly. We must stand firm, dear friend. These are only our first disappointments, I'm afraid. God will in due course desire that everything let go of us, so that we will be able to find support only in him, that is to say, in our awareness of Good and Evil, of what is just and unjust, which he has put in us. Catholics have little by little lost the use of their conscience, or else they still use it, if at all, only to resolve little problems of private behavior, and to do so hesitantly and almost always in the direction of their own interests. The freedom which the Church leaves us is a positive value, a positive right, which it is our duty to use for God's glory, instead of burying it like the talent in the gospel. There is a risk in this, to be sure. But blind obedience too, outside the religious state, is risky. There is risk in everything. And you have to take this risk humbly upon yourself. The virtue of fortitude has been given us for that.

Most cordially yours,
Georges Bernanos

Letter to a Young Worker

La Pinède, Bandol (Var) (April 1946?)

Dear Sir,

I would like to dedicate more time to you, but I have a lot of work; I'm over my head—and heart—in work . . . Pardon me, and bear in mind that I have to support nine people—big and small—with this work. In God's name, and with his grace, it is a poor Christian's lot to give exactly what he doesn't have. What would become of love otherwise, where would be the sweet miracle of love? . . .

You see, it is very difficult to proceed as you request, by a series of questions and answers, as the Church herself does when she determines error by approving or condemning certain propositions . . . *Anathema sit!* . . . You say to me: *We feel you are right.* Yes, indeed, that's exactly it: the operation of the mind we call judgment. We must either get to the point where we *feel we are right* or we must resign ourselves to having eternal discussions with ourselves, as the poor damned souls in hell must have with the greatest logician of them all, whose name is the devil. Every comprehensive judgment is a risk, a wager. But the superstition, or rather, the idolatry called Technology, closes our eyes to the divinatory character of Reason, which must either make a *choice* at the right moment or resign itself to a perpetual condition of *doing without.*

Culture is bankrupt, that is beyond doubt. But it didn't come to this point suddenly, as the result of a miscalculation. You can follow the trail that led it here. The modern collective state already opposes us Christians in the same way the pagan state did, and it will eliminate us for the same reasons. It seems to me that there is an invaluable criterion of discernment here. At bottom, this world wants only comfort, comfort no matter what the cost, and in order to fool others and itself, it declares that this comfort is actually justice. We don't dare contradict this, because we would have to appeal to the dogma of original sin, which deprived us of the right to the happiness that the first man enjoyed, and Mr. Barbu's constituents wouldn't stomach that. They wouldn't stand for being reminded that when the gospel calls us to seek first the kingdom and the righteousness of God it means HIS kingdom and HIS righteousness. When we seek happiness first, under the pretext that, after all, we might as well begin sometime, then humanly speaking we're not reasoning badly: but we are reasoning as if the Messiah had come to reopen to us the gates of the earthly paradise; we are reasoning just like the Jews. We are getting ready to crucify the Lord again, under the pretext that he isn't living up to our earthly expectations, that a scourged and crucified Messiah who summons us to get scourged and crucified with him can hardly be the true Messiah. To be sure, this doesn't mean that we should turn away indifferently from men's happiness, quite the contrary! We must even—at the great risk of being treated as enemies of the human race, like our fathers in the faith—call their attention to the fact that sooner or later they will become slaves of the colossal machine for universal happiness that they have erected against God like a new Tower of Babel. For there is a certain misery and injustice in the world that we cannot touch without simultaneously risking the annihilation of man's freedom. What is the proof of that? Revelation. If we don't bear witness to the truths of revelation, what is the point of still calling ourselves Christians? And though in the end events would infallibly prove that revelation is right, our risk and our honor lie precisely in sacrificing our reputation and our life so that Evil won't be pushed too far. After all, the good Lord didn't send us out among the peoples simply in order to announce inevitable catastrophe to them: "I told you so!"

The universal system of the planned economy leads to totalitarianism, that is, to the profound and irrevocable dethronement of the human society that refuses to risk, that is unwilling to put everything on the line. Man was driven *as man* out of the earthly paradise, but he gets around the barrier by slipping in again *as an animal.* Our duty consists in announcing to him that he is going to fail miserably in this undertaking, that the atom bomb—the genuine "blitzkrieg" in the strict sense of the word—should serve him as a warning. Man will destroy himself before he succeeds in transforming himself into the *homo oeconomicus* whom Marxism needs for its planetary factory. Can what I am laying out here be proved like $2 \times 2 = 4$? Of course not. But if you have the courage to lead a life of prayer, then you already know from experience that God has shortcuts for helping us arrive at certain truths of salvation, that there is a kind of fourth dimension where reason can move with the rapidity of lightning. Alas, we know how to use our souls as little as we do our bodies. We are equally ignorant of both.

I find Barbu's experiment extremely interesting. My only fear is that it comes too late. A Marxist state (socialist or communist) won't permit it. It's much too dangerous. But the French could try it *outside* of France.

Concerning your possible departure, to Brazil for example, I hope that I can be useful to you one day. But I am waiting until events—that is, the will of God—allow me a clear view. I have grand plans—grand in relation to my modest person! . . . I still don't know whether they can be carried through or not. I won't attempt to carry them out until I believe I am certain of having no better means of serving my country. Be assured that I will be thinking of you then, as I will of so many others, known and unknown, whom I truly carry in my heart. Until then don't be too burdensome on your good poor wives, who already have enough to do to keep you from starving to death.

If you have the chance to get yourself René Gillouin's *Aristarchie*, read it. Unfortunately it came out in Geneva (*Éditions du Cheval ailé*), with Constant Bourquin, Geneva. I would like to give you something else to read: *L'evolution régressive*. I'll try to get a copy sent to you.

Sermon of an Agnostic on the Feast of St. Thérèse[1]

The world shall be judged by children. The spirit of childhood shall judge the world.

Of course, the Saint of Lisieux never wrote anything of the kind. Maybe she never had any precise idea of the wondrous spring of which she was the herald. She can hardly have expected, I mean, that one day it would stretch over the earth, and that sweet-smelling tides and snow-white foam would cover towns of steel and reinforced concrete, innocent fields in their terror of mechanical monsters, and even the black soaked soil of death. "I shall bring forth a shower of roses," she said, twenty years before 1914.

But she didn't know what roses they would be.

*   *   *

You know, sometimes I imagine what any decent agnostic of average intelligence might say, if by some impossible chance one of those intolerable praters were to let him stand awhile in the pulpit, in his stead, on the day consecrated to Saint Thérèse of Lisieux, for instance:

"Ladies and gentlemen," he would begin, "I don't share your beliefs, but I probably know more about the history of the Church than you do, because I happen to have read it,

---

1. Translated by Pamela Morris and David Louis Schindler, Jr. [David Christopher Schindler –Ed.]

and not many parishioners can say that. (If I'm wrong, let those who have signify in the usual manner.)

"Ladies and gentlemen, it is well and good to praise the saints as you do, and I am grateful to the priest for allowing me to join in your praising. The saints belong more to you than to me, because you worship the same Master. There's nothing strange about your congratulating yourselves for the glory they've won by their extraordinary lives, but—pardon the observation—I find it hard to believe that they would have endured such struggle and strife only so that you could have such celebrations; celebrations, moreover, that exclude the thousands of poor devils who have never heard of these heroes, and who will never hear of them except for you alone.

"True, every year the Postal Service circulates calendars with the saints' names inscribed alongside the phases of the moon. Indeed, these sublime squanderers have given up everything, even their names, which that other vigilant administration, namely the civil state, has put at the disposal of all comers, believer and unbeliever alike, to serve in the registry for newborn citizens. As for the rest of us, we don't know the saints—and it seems as though you don't know them much more than we do. Who among you is capable of writing twenty lines about his or her patron saint? There was a time when such ignorance puzzled me; now, it seems as normal to me as it does to you.

"Well now, I know you're not inclined to worry much about what people of my sort think. And the most pious among you are even very anxious to avoid all discussion with infidels, in case they were to 'lose their faith,' as they put it. All I can say is their 'faith' must be hanging by a thread. It makes you wonder what the faith of the lukewarm can be! We often call such poor creatures shams and hypocrites; but we can't help feeling rather sad about it all.

For though you're not interested in unbelievers, unbelievers are extremely interested in you. There are few of us who at some point in our lives have not made a tentative approach in your direction, were it only to insult you. After all, put yourselves in our place. Were there but one chance, the smallest chance, the faintest chance of you being right, death would come as a devastating surprise to us. So we're bound to watch you closely and try to fathom you. You're supposed to believe in hell. So I think that when you look upon us, your comrades on earth, it might at least be with a fragment of compassion, such as you would not refuse to anyone serving a life-sentence here. Mind you, we're not expecting any ridiculous demonstrations, but still the very thought of your dance-partners, bridge-partners, holiday companions going to grind their teeth and curse their Maker for all eternity—surely that ought to have some effect on you.

"Yes, we were drawn to you. But now we've decided that you're not very interesting after all, and it's rather disappointing. And we hate to think what fools we were, ever to have hoped in you, and to have doubted ourselves, our own unbelief.

"Most of the people like me rest content with their initial impression. This impression, however, doesn't resolve a thing, for there are clearly among you many insincere Christians who are interesting precisely on account of their instability. But the others remain. Anyone who were to watch them couldn't fail to notice that, though the faith they profess makes little difference in their lives—since they indulge in moderate doses of six of the deadly sins just like everyone else—it poisons their pathetic pleasures by the extreme importance it attaches to the seventh, presumed to be 'mortal.'

"My dear brothers, when you are not possessed of that

heroism without which Léon Bloy says a Christian is no more than a pig, it is by the neurotic quality of your lust that you are instantly recognizable. You must really believe in hell. You fear it for yourselves. You expect it for us.

"How amazing that in the circumstances you are so entirely lacking in pathos!

"Christian ladies and Christian gentlemen, if ever you were to be filmed unawares, you would be staggered to see on the screen an entirely different person to the motionless double in your mirror. In the same way it is possible that by dint of examination of conscience you have gradually discovered in yourself qualities which with time have grown so familiar to you, that you innocently believe everybody can see them. But we can't see your consciences! On the other hand, your vocabulary is within our reach far more than you are—though for you the meaning has doubtless been weakened by long use. And it makes us wonder! What about that mysterious expression: in a state of grace? When you come out of the confessional, you're 'in a state of grace.' A state of grace . . . are you sure? Can you blame us if we don't believe it? We're wondering what you do with the Grace of God. Should it not be shining out of you? Where the devil do you hide your joy?

"You'll say that's none of my business. If such joy were given me, I wouldn't know what to do with it. Perhaps. You generally talk in that acid, revengeful way, as though you hated us for the pleasures of which you have deprived yourselves. Can they be so precious in your eyes? Alas, we don't think so much of them. You seem to take us for animals who find in exercising their functions of digestion or reproduction, a source of inexhaustible delight, ever renewed, ever fresh, as though such indulgences were forgotten the instant they were over.

"But I assure you the vanity of vanities has no more secrets for us. The most bitter verses in the Book of Job or Ecclesiastes can teach us nothing we don't already know, and they have already inspired our poets and painters. If you will give the matter thought, I think you will agree that we are rather like the men of the Old Testament. The modern world is as harsh as the Jewish world, and its incessant clamor is the same as that heard by the Prophets, thrown up to the skies from huge cities along the waterside. The silence of death is haunting us also, and we answer it, as they did, by cries of hate and of terror.

"And we worship the same calf. To worship a Calf is not, I assure you, the sign of an optimistic people. We are corroded by the same leprosy of which Semitic imagination bears the hideous wound throughout the centuries: the obsession of nothingness, the impotence—almost physical impotence—to conceive of the Resurrection. Even in the days of Our Lord, with the exception of the small community of Pharisees, the Jewish people had little faith in future life. Perhaps they yearned for it too much—a yearning from the loins, which devours us too. Christian hope never quenches a thirst of that kind, we know. Hope slips through us, as through a sieve. You may say that Israel was awaiting the Messiah. We are awaiting ours. And in the same way again, we are not too sure of his advent: and for fear, also, of seeing our last illusion fly away from us, we rope it firmly to the ground; we dream of a carnal Messiah: Science, Progress, by which we should become masters of the Earth.

"Yes, we are men of the Old Testament. You may say that in such case our blindness is even more culpable than theirs. I disagree. In the first place, there is not reason to suppose that we should have crucified the Savior. You cannot get away from the fact that Deicides are of the edifying class.

You may say what you like, and try all you can to get away from it, but Deicide can never again be regarded as a crime for the rabble. It is a most distinguished, a very unusual crime reserved for opulent priests, sanctioned by the powerful middle class and the intellectuals. (In those days they were called scribes.)

"You may snicker, my dear brothers, but it isn't the Communists and Blasphemers who crucified Our Lord. And forgive me if I have a good laugh, too. You naturally consider the New Testament inspired, you lay emphasis on each verse of that Holy Book, and can you never have been really struck by the insistence of Jesus on generally white-washing a class of persons, who—to say the least—could hardly have been described as judges, solicitors, retired generals (not forgetting their virtuous spouses) nor even—between ourselves—as the clergy? Aren't you a little disturbed by the fact that God should have reserved His most stringent maledictions for some of the very 'best' people, regular church-goers, never missing a fasting day, and far better instructed in their religion—excepting yourselves of course—than the majority of parishioners today? Doesn't such a huge paradox attract your attention? We can't help noticing it, you know.

"It is no answer to say that God has entrusted Himself into your hands. The hands in which Christ entrusted Himself, of yore, were not friendly hands: they were consecrated. That you should have succeeded to the Synagogue, and that such succession should be legitimate, is of no consequence.

"We are waiting to share with you a gift which you proclaim to be priceless, and we don't want to know whether God entrusted Himself to you; we want to know what you are doing with Him!

* * *

"My dear brothers and sisters, I can see from here the imperious profile of Colonel Romorantin. He is talking with Mr. Mortgage-holder and several of the clerks familiar to this parish, which is now filled with indignant looks. 'This is our parish, after all! This gentleman has never been introduced to us; I do not know him, and he takes advantage of that fact to tell us unpleasant things.' But, my dear Colonel, your Church, after all, is no military society! It would bring me joy to see you take up your throne beneath the vast cupola of the Church Triumphant, but for the time being you are only a candidate like everyone else. Are we celebrating the feast of St. Thérèse or that of the parishioners? To watch you take your place in the choir, I would think I was watching a new academician being received by his uniformed colleagues. One would think that the sublime doctrine of the Communion of Saints merely adds another prerogative to your already long list. But isn't this doctrine complemented by that of the reversibility of merits? We, the rest of us, answer only for our actions or their material consequences. The solidarity that binds you to others is of a much higher sort. As I see it, the gift of faith that was bestowed upon you, far from granting you freedom, has bound you to them by bonds stronger than flesh and blood.

"You are the salt of the earth. If the world loses its flavor, who is it I should blame? It is no use to boast of the merits won by your saints, since you are first of all only the stewards of these goods. We often hear the best among you proclaim with pride that they 'owe nothing to anyone.' Coming from your mouths, such words are utterly senseless, for you are literally indebted to everyone, to each of us, to me myself.

It is possible, Colonel, that you are riddled with more debts than a junior lieutenant! God alone is privy to our treasuries. If it is true, as your priests say, that the fate of one who holds earthly power may depend, as we speak, on the will of a child torn between good and evil, and who resists grace with all of his feeble strength, nothing is more ludicrous than hearing you speak about the affairs of this world in the most casual tones! Oh, what strange people you are!

"Colonel Romorantin will no doubt say tonight, as he is shuffling the cards, 'What does he mean by that nonsense? My gosh, all of us in this family are implicit believers!' For your morality is ultimately no different from anyone else's: what you call sin is just given a different name by the moralists. Ah, yes! What curious characters you are! When you hear tell that a tiny Carmelite girl with tuberculosis was able, through the heroic practice of duties as humble as she is herself, to obtain the conversion of thousands, or even—why not!—the victory of 1918, you show no sign of contradiction. But if, on the other hand, one were to say to you in all politeness that, according to your own logic the corruption of the Mexican clergy, for example, is the supernatural cause of the persecutions in this unfortunate country, you shrug your shoulders: 'How could there be any relation between the greed, avarice, or concubinage of those poor priests, and the bloody crimes perpetrated by such monsters here?'

"This reasoning is valid for everyone else in the world, but not for you. This is the reasoning of the judges of this world who punish the adulterer with a five-dollar fine and lock a beggar away for six months for petty theft. Similarly, you see sense in the claim that the Curé of Ars was able to draw his countryfolk to Mass because of a lifestyle so destitute that his confreres even considered sending the poor man away. But if I had the misfortune of insinuating that Fr.

So-and-so from Spain, though perfectly in line with his country's tribunals, might nevertheless be the spiritual father of a parish of murders and sacrilege, I would almost certainly be dealt the Bolshevik treatment. Are all of you imbeciles, or are you just pretending? One might easily overlook the fact that your faith is without works. Because we do not believe in the efficacy of your sacraments, we could reproach you for not being better than us only if we were motivated by spite. But what surpasses the understanding is that you habitually reason about the affairs of this world in exactly the same way we do. I mean, who's forcing you? That you act according to our principles, or rather, according to the hard experience of men who, having no hope in another world, fight like animals and plants in this one according to the laws of survival—so be it. But when your fathers profess the pitiless economics of Mr. Adam Smith, or when you give solemn honor to Machiavelli, allow me to say that you cause us no surprise—you simply strike us as queer, incomprehensible fellows.

"This sincere disquisition will not, I know, shake the solid optimism that you give the name 'hope,' no doubt by analogy. The problem with supernatural virtues is that they have to be practiced with heroism. Things stand with them as they stand with those people who rise to the occasion when provoked, but who are for all of that more easily seduced. Humility dampens the mighty. Cleverly co-opted, the virtue of humility can spare the mediocre the horrors of humiliation, or at least sweeten its bitterness. When circumstances force us to admit that we are not worth the space we occupy, what can we do but close our eyes to such painful evidence? We do not always succeed. To admit to oneself that one is a weakling, a liar or a scoundrel is hardly comforting to people of our ilk. And yet, when some of you undertake this exercise, you manifest a certain satisfaction that strikes us as somewhat comical. By no grace of God, you read an act of humility in the missalette and come through beaming with self-admiration. Such an operation seems a little too self-serving to be something truly supernatural.

* * *

"Dear friends, I'm afraid my exordium is getting on your nerves. But I was distressed by your bad opinion of us, and I am doing my best to make you revise it. I don't think your opinion is thought out, or deliberate. You see unbelievers as they are, and Christians as they should be—an unfortunate misapprehension. Or rather you see us as indeed we should be, if you were Christians, according to the spirit of the New Testament. For then you would have had the right to condemn our callousness. But do you think it is exactly pleasant to be described daily as the enemies of God by folk so highly supernatural as yourselves? Such a qualification didn't matter very much to our fathers or grandfathers, in the days when your orators were continually invoking against us the sacred rights of freedom of conscience. But for us it might mean the regrettable solicitude of a crusading general.

"No, dear brothers, many unbelievers are not as hardened as you imagine. Need I remind you that God came in Person to the Jewish people. They saw Him. They heard Him. Their hands touched Him. They asked for signs; He gave them those signs. He healed the sick and raised the dead. Then He ascended once again to the Heavens. When we seek Him now, in this world, it is you we find, and only you. Oh, I respect the Church—but the history of the Church herself, after all, does not surrender its secret to the first-comer. There is Rome—but you know that the greatness of Catholicism is not immediately apparent, and many of you yourselves come back disappointed. What do you expect from us? It is you, Christians, who participate in divinity as your liturgy proclaims; it is you, 'divine men,' who ever since His Ascension have been His representatives on earth.

"Well, you must admit that one would hardly know it at first glance!

* * *

"You probably find these observations misplaced, here, within these walls. They are no more misplaced than the presence of most of you. They are certainly quite unworthy of the saint whose feast we celebrate, but they at least have the merit of being simple—even childish. The smile I see from Mr. Mortgage-holder is a sure witness of that fact.

"The Saint whose festival it is this day will not mind my speaking as a child. For I am but a child grown old and burdened with inexperience, and you haven't much to fear from me. Fear those who are to come, who shall judge you. Fear the innocence of children, for they are also *enfants terribles*. Your only way out is to become children yourselves, to rediscover the heart of childhood. For the hour shall strike when questions hurled at you from all points of the earth shall be so urgent and so direct, that you will not be able to answer except by yes or no. The society in which you live seems more complex than others because of its talent for complicating problems, or at least for presenting them under a thousand and one aspects, a talent that allows it to invent by turns provisional solutions which it naturally presents as definitive. Such has been the method in medicine since the time of Molière. But it is likewise now the method followed by economists and sociologists.

"I maintain that you hold an advantageous place in this society, because, by calling itself materialistic, it allows you at small cost the immense privilege of criticizing it in the name of the Spirit. Unfortunately for you, beyond a certain degree of guile and deception, the most insolent of phraseologies cannot mask the void of systems. When a professor hears a particular murmur slowly rising in a hall, barely perceptible as yet, if he piles on authority and gravity, that supreme effort will be his final downfall. You may have read, for example, the following lines that appeared in one of the recent issues of the *Revue de Paris*, authored by a Mr. Paul Morand: 'I can very easily imagine the autarchies of tomorrow prescribing celibacy in certain ill-favored regions, and on the other hand promoting births in more valuable districts, according to some vast embryogenic strategy. After having regulated the quantity of births, the future State will of course focus on the quality—not wanting to remain on this side of the modern State, the director of breeding.' Mr. Paul Morand belongs to the highest society; he is in fact a professional. There are thus no grounds for thinking him a humorist. Since, as far as I can tell, Mr. Patenôtre is no humorist himself, his recent testimonial could be heard by an audience as serious as the one I presently have the honor of addressing:

> Let us imagine a collectivity as rich as the United States, or even as Great Britain or France, in which we wiped clean any prejudices, *tabula rasa*, and we decided unanimously one fine day to maximize production without regard for the demands of clientele. At once, the factories would

perfect their equipment and would run it, day and night, under rotating personnel; likewise, in rural areas, the production of grains, market crops, and livestock would increase their yield.

What would be the result? The volume of this agricultural and industrial production, after so many years, would reach such dimensions that we might reasonably imagine a just distribution capable of granting each and every human being a significant comfort-level and a high standard of living.

Why, then, must the routine of our methods and the straightjacket of our prejudices oppose the march of progress, halting this high standard of living with the cry, "Thou shall not pass!"? What foul element must thus infect our economic system, imprisoning it in a vicious circle, in which production is restrained by insufficiently solvent consumption, while this rate of consumption is in turn rendered insufficiently solvent, primarily through limited production?

"I don't know if you appreciate as well as I do the naivete of this confession. So much energy wasted in creating a self-proclaimed materialistic society that is no longer capable of either producing or selling! You must admit that, in these conditions, the men of order, of a certain order, can dress up in red, in yellow, or in green, dictators can grind their teeth and show the whites of their eyes, and, nevertheless, the kids whose parents have trained them at the theater will begin to exchange glances—having found their Punch and Judy once again!—and the hall will founder in peals of laughter.

"Christians who listen to me—that is your peril! It is difficult to follow upon a society that has foundered in laughter, because even the fragments will be useless. You will have to build it all up again. You will have to build it up under the eyes of children. Become as children yourselves. They have found the chink in your armor, and you will never disarm their irony save by simplicity, honesty, and audacity.

"You will never disarm them save by heroism.

*   *   *

"In speaking thus, I don't think I am betraying the inspiration of Saint Thérèse of Lisieux. I am simply interpreting it. I am trying to turn it to some human use in the affairs of the world. She preached the spirit of Childhood. The spirit of Childhood is capable of both good and evil. It is not the spirit of resignation to injustice. Nor must you make of it the spirit of revolt, for it would sweep you off the earth.

"This surmise in no way comforts me, for we should be swept too . . .

"For your history, the history of the Church, seems at first only to add a single chapter to History. But this is not at all the case. The prudence and folly of men may be inscribed, one after the other, in the book of history, and still they will never wholly account for the successes and failures. But I know such a thing is not evident at first glance! Moreover, it matters not for example whether one took down, page after page, in basically equivalent proportions, all manner of known errors. I believe that they would not follow upon each other according to any law, that they would not follow the same order of consequence. You explain such singularities through divine assistance. I shall not contradict you on this point. I think, for example, short of being a fool, no one could remain oblivious to the extraordinary quality of your heroes, to their incomparable humanity. Moreover, the name 'hero' is scarcely appropriate for them, and the name 'genius' rings false as well, for the saints are at once heroes and geniuses. But heroism and genius typically occur only at the expense of a certain human quality, while the humanity of your saints abounds. I would thus say that they are at once heroes, geniuses and children. What great fortune! I don't mind telling you, we would rather deal with them than with you. But, alas, experience has taught us that all direct contact with them is impossible. What do you think our politicians or moralists would do with a Thérèse of Lisieux? Her message coming from their mouths would lose all meaning, or at least any chance at producing an effect. It was written in your language, and your language alone can express it. We lack the words necessary to translate it without betraying it, and that's all there is to it. My dear brothers and sisters, I make this confession in all humility—please receive it in the same spirit. For if it is you alone who are able to transmit the message of the saints; it is, alas! necessary that you be the ones responsible for fulfilling this obligation in our regard. I'm sorry to have to tell you that we pay dearly for your neglect.

"And do not try to tell us that these divine human beings came only to add a few finishing touches to the painting. Take, for instance, the message of Saint Francis. This—if you will forgive my presumption—is what he might have said: 'Things are going badly, my children—very badly. And they're going to get a lot worse. I wish I could be more reassuring regarding the state of your health. But if beef-tea was all you required, I'd have stayed quietly at home, for I was very fond of my friends, and I used to accompany myself on the lute, and sing southern songs to them in the evenings. Salvation is within your reach. But it's no good shirking the issue, for there is only one, and it is called Poverty. I am not bringing up the rear, my children, I am preceding you. I am rushing ahead—don't be so frightened. If I were able to suffer alone, you may be sure I wouldn't have interfered with your amusements. But, alas, God does not allow it. You have incensed my Lady Poverty. You have provoked her beyond endurance; because she is so patient, you have subtly, gradually, lifted your entire burden on to her shoulders. Now she lies, always in silence, with her face to the ground, and weeping in the dust. And you think: there's nothing more to get in our way—on with the dance! But you are not going to dance, my children, you are going to die . . . The malediction of Poverty means death. Follow me!'

"That advice was addressed to all of you. But not many followed it. You are rather like the legendary Italian soldiers waiting to attack. All of a sudden the colonel snatches up his saber, jumps over the parapet, and charges off beneath heavy fire, all by himself, crying *Avanti! Avanti!* Whilst his soldiers remain crouching under cover, electrified by such a display of valor, clapping loudly, with tears in their eyes: *Bravo! Bravo! Bravissimo!*

"My dear brothers, I keep on saying the same thing, because it always is the same thing. Had you followed that Saint instead of applauding, Europe would never have known the Reformation, nor the religious wars, nor this horrible Spanish Crusade. Saint Francis was calling to you, but death did not pick and choose: death descended on us all. The danger is the same today. It must be even greater.

The Saint of Lisieux, whose prodigious career is sufficient token in itself of the tragic urgency of the message entrusted to her, asks you to become as children. The purpose of God is impenetrable, as you say. Yet I cannot help feeling that this is your last chance. Your last chance—and ours. Are you capable of rejuvenating our world or not?

"The New Testament is eternally young, it is you who are so old. And your 'old men' are even older than the oldest of you. They go wagging their heads and mumbling: 'We don't want either Fascists or Communists,' in voices so hollow and cracked that they spew out a tooth at every syllable. Reaction is essential, and we could do with a revolution! But not all your reactions and revolutions put together would suffice. God, can't you forget your decrepit scruple of preserving an order which no longer spares itself, which is destroying itself? Besides, universal order has been replaced by general mobilization. Call back your casuists, before they get mobilized too! Call 'em back, or rather—take 'em away. For the poor things have been indulging in such involved contortions that their legs are round their necks, and their arms are dug into their shoulders, and their heads are on a level with their lowest vertebrae. Carry them home just as they are, on your stretchers, for they'll never get unknotted by themselves.

"Nothing has been really lost in these two thousand years of useless negotiations, for the New Testament has reached us intact, not a comma missing. Is it therefore so hard merely to answer yes or no to all future questions? Men of honor talk thus. Honor belongs also to childhood. Because it is based on childhood, it is able to escape the analysis of moralists, for your moralist only torments the 'mature' fabulous creatures which he has invented for the convenience of his own deductions. There are no mature men, there is no intermediary state between one age and the next. Whoever cannot give more than he receives will surely fall to dust. What morality or physiology has to say regarding such a factor of great importance is of no consequence to us, because we give to the words of youth and age an entirely different meaning. The knowledge of men—and not the experience of men—soon teaches us that youth and age are a matter of character, or soul, if you prefer. A kind of predestination. You will agree that these views are no innovation. The most obtuse observer knows perfectly well that a miser is old at twenty.

"There is a country of the Young. That country is calling to you, that country must be saved. Do not wait for the country of the Old to finish destroying it by those same methods which, in less than a century, not so long ago, defeated the Redskins. You must not let the Young be colonized by the Old! Don't imagine that your words are sufficient protection—even when they get printed. In the days when the American Pharisees were methodically exterminating a race a thousand times more precious than their own foul conglomeration, did not the sham Indians of Chateaubriand and Cooper share with the sham Scots of Walter Scott, the cozy leisure of romantically minded old maids, wallowing in pity, as in freshly spilt blood? The advent of Joan of Arc in the twentieth century has the character of a solemn warning. The remarkable fate of an obscure little Carmelite girl seems to me an even more serious sign.

"Christians, hurry up and become children again, that we may become children too. It can't be so very difficult. Because you do not live your faith, your faith has ceased to be a living thing. It has become abstract—bodyless. Perhaps we shall find that the disincarnation of the word of God is the real cause of all our misfortune. Many of you use the truths of the New Testament as initial themes out of which you compose a kind of orchestral variation inspired by worldly wisdom. In your endeavor to justify these truths in the eyes of political doctrinaires, are you not afraid of placing them beyond the reach of simple men? Why not—just for once—oppose them, just as they are, to our complicated systems, and then wait, quietly wait for the answer, without talking all the time?

"Joan of Arc was but a girl-saint, yet she put the Paris Doctors of Divinity in a tight spot. Why not let the Christ-Child have His say? You may suggest that's none of my business. I beg your pardon: to get the better of an order almost as petrified as ours, so many Doctors were unnecessary! That is a historical fact of great significance. I quite understand that you should be attached to your libraries. They have been of great use against arch-heretics. But the world is not merely being poisoned by arch-heretics, it is obsessed by the idea of suicide. From one end of the planet to the other, it is hurriedly piling up all the necessary adjuncts to this gigantic enterprise. You won't snatch a man from suicide by proving to him that suicide is anti-social, because the poor devil is planning to desert, by means of death, a society which disgusts him. And you go on urging men, in a manner barely distinct from the Moralists—the Morality-Machines—to check their desires! But they have no desires! They have no longer any purposes. They can discover none that is worth an effort.

"Christian Ladies and Christian Gentlemen, I am coming to the end of my long harangue. As an agnostic, I regret being unable to give you my blessing. I remain your very humble servant. To feel much as you do, almost as disconcerted as yourselves in face of these formidable times, is just a little heart-rending. Because, forgive my frankness if I say that you are just as anxious to save your skins as we are. The slogan of crazy despair—never mind what happens so long as I get out!—is about to be shaped on your lips, whilst your eyes steal glances at Dictatorships. Anybody, anyhow! What the hell! Get back to childhood, it's not so dangerous.

"We're bound to say that we haven't the slightest confidence in your political capacity. Soon your excess of zeal will have compromised you, even with your new masters. To become the pet aversion of free men, and of the poor, with a program like the New Testament, is rather ludicrous, don't you agree? Become as little children—there lies your refuge. And when the Powerful of the world ask you insidious questions about all kinds of dangerous problems, such as 'modern warfare,' 'the respect of treaties,' 'capitalistic organization,' don't be ashamed to confess that you're too foolish to make any reply, and that Lord Jesus shall answer for you.

"For then the word of God may perhaps work the miracle of rallying together men of good will, since it is for them that it was spoken. *Pax hominibus bonae voluntatis* could hardly be translated into: 'First we'll have a war, and we'll see later,' could it?

"I know it is a paradox for us to be awaiting a miracle. But it would be an even greater paradox to await it from you. Therefore we take precautions. We feel we have every right because, mind you, we do not claim to interpret the New Testament, we call upon you to carry it out, according to your belief, and the belief of your Church. We do not refute your learned doctors. We refute your political meddlers, because they have given us abundant proof of their presumption and stupidity. The Gospel! The Gospel! When finally you stake everything on a miracle, it is only natural to insist that the experiment should be faultlessly carried out.

"Supposing, my brothers, that I were consumptive, and I

wished to drink the waters of Lourdes, and doctors suggested that they should dilute in it some drug of their own. 'My dear doctors,' I would reply, 'you have said I was incurable. Let me try my luck undisturbed. In this matter, which is strictly between myself and Our Lady, if I need any go-between, you can be sure I won't be asking the pharmacist.'"

www.ingramcontent.com/pod-product-compliance
Lightning Source LLC
Chambersburg PA
CBHW050334120526
44592CB00014B/2178